ALBUM OF SONATINAS FOR YOUNG FLUTISTS

In Progressive Order

BY CLEMENTI · KUHLAU · J.C. BACH · BEETHOVEN · MOZART · SCHUBERT · TELEMANN

Transcribed and Adapted for
Flute and Piano by Louis Moyse

ED-2304

ISBN 978-0-7935-5212-2

G. SCHIRMER, Inc.

DISTRIBUTED BY

HAL•LEONARD®
CORPORATION

7777 W. BLUEMOUND RD. P.O. BOX 13819 MILWAUKEE, WI 53213

CONTENTS

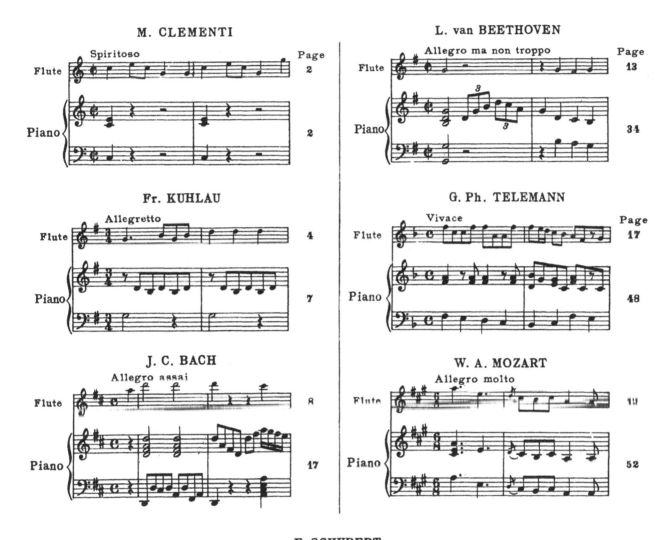

Album of Sonatinas
in Progressive Order
for Young Flutists

Transcribed and adapted by
Louis Moyse

Sonatina

Muzio Clementi Op. 36, No. 1
(1752–1832)

44374

Sonatina

Friedrich Kuhlau Op. 55, No. 2
(1786-1832)

Sonatina

Johann Christian Bach
(1735-1782)

44374

Andante grazioso

Sonatina

Ludwig van Beethoven Op. 49, No. 2
(1770 - 1827)

Allegro ma non troppo

Tempo di minuetto

44

ALBUM OF SONATINAS FOR YOUNG FLUTISTS
In Progressive Order

Transcribed and Adapted for
Flute and Piano by Louis Moyse

CONTENTS

ED-2304
ISBN 978-0-7935-5212-2

G. SCHIRMER, Inc.

DISTRIBUTED BY

Hal•Leonard® CORPORATION
7777 W. BLUEMOUND RD. P.O. BOX 13819 MILWAUKEE, WI 53213

Album of Sonatinas
in Progressive Order
for Young Flutists

Flute

Transcribed and adapted by
Louis Moyse

Sonatina

Muzio Clementi Op. 36, No. 1
(1752-1832)

Spiritoso

Andante

44374 Cx

Vivace

Sonatina

Friedrich Kuhlau Op. 55, No. 2
(1786-1832)

Flute

Flute

Sonatina

Johann Christian Bach
(1735-1782)

Allegro assai

Flute

Flute

Sonatina

Ludwig van Beethoven Op. 49, No. 2
(1770-1827)

Allegro ma non troppo

44374

Flute

Sonatina

Georg Philipp Telemann
(1681 - 1767)

Sonatina
(K. 305)

Flute

Wolfgang Amadeus Mozart
(1756-1791)

Flute

44374

Tema con variazioni
Andante grazioso

Var. III

Allegro

Flute
Sonatina

Franz Schubert, Op. 137, No. 1
(1797-1828)

Flute

Flute

Flute

44374

Flute

Sonatina

Georg Philipp Telemann
(1681-1767)

Cantabile

Presto

Sonatina
(K. 305)

Wolfgang Amadeus Mozart
(1756-1791)

Allegro molto

44374

Tema con variazioni
Andante grazioso

Var. I

Var. II

Var. III
Allegro

Sonatina

Franz Schubert, Op. 137, No. 1
(1797-1828)